K-POP'S BIG WAVE

K-POP'S BIG WAVE

A Global Phenomenon

Sarah Roggio

LERNER PUBLICATIONS ◆ MINNEAPOLIS

Lerner Publications Company
An imprint of Lerner Publishing Group, Inc.
241 First Avenue North
Minneapolis, MN 55401 USA

For reading levels and more information, look up this title at www.lernerbooks.com.

Main body text set in ITC Garamond Std Book.
Typeface provided by Adobe Systems.

Editor: Annie Zheng **Designer:** Lauren Cooper

Library of Congress Cataloging-in-Publication Data

Names: Roggio, Sarah, author.
Title: K-pop's big wave : a global phenomenon / Sarah Roggio.
Description: Minneapolis : Lerner Publications, 2026. | Series: Gateway headlines | Includes bibliographical references and index. | Audience: Ages 9–14 | Audience: Grades 4–6 | Summary: "Around the world, K-pop has exploded in popularity thanks to groups such as BTS, BLACKPINK, Stray Kids, and more. Readers discover the history of K-pop and its global impact on music, entertainment, and daily life"— Provided by publisher.
Identifiers: LCCN 2025013349 (print) | LCCN 2025013350 (ebook) | ISBN 9798765689561 (library binding) | ISBN 9798348028640 (paperback) | ISBN 9798765695340 (epub)
Subjects: LCSH: Popular music—Korea (South)—History and criticism—Juvenile literature. | Musicians—Korea (South)—Juvenile literature. | K-pop (Subculture)—Juvenile literature.
Classification: LCC ML3502.K6 R64 2026 (print) | LCC ML3502.K6 (ebook) | DDC 781.63095195—dc23/eng/20250512

LC record available at https://lccn.loc.gov/2025013349
LC ebook record available at https://lccn.loc.gov/2025013350

Manufactured in the United States of America
1-1012827-54824-8/12/2025

Table of Contents

BLACKPINK attends the red carpet event for the theatrical release of the group's BORN PINK World Tour in 2024.

In November 2024 singers Rosé and Bruno Mars exploded onto the stage at the 2024 Mnet Asian Music Awards (MAMA) show. They wore matching baggy suits and sang in Korean and English. They synchronized their steps to the song's bouncy beat. Bruno Mars's backup band, The Hooligans, joined in the fun. Excited fans jumped along through the entire song. They clapped and chanted the catchy chorus. They were singing the K-pop collaboration "APT," which smashed music records worldwide.

Rosé wore a black-and-pink tie. These are the colors of her K-pop group BLACKPINK. Rosé released an album on her own in 2024, which included the song "APT." She wrote the song's lyrics based on the chant "APT" from a South Korean hand-clapping game. Bruno Mars helped polish the music for the song, which blends rap, pop,

Bruno Mars is a Grammy Award-winning artist known for hits such as "Die with a Smile" and "When I Was Your Man."

and punk music. "It's so straightforward and hooks you instantly," music critic Cha Woo-jin said. "All the kids are singing along to it, which is a big deal because it appeals across ages."

"APT" came out in October 2024. It became the fastest K-pop music video to get over one billion views on YouTube. Fans created viral TikTok dances to celebrate the song. Rosé also earned a Guinness World Record for "APT." She became the first K-pop artist to reach number one on Apple Music's Top 100 Global Chart.

The 2024 MAMA show began at the Dolby Theatre in Los Angeles, California. "APT" won MAMA's 2024 global sensation award. South Korea's MAMA shows are one of K-pop's most important ceremonies. The "APT" performance marked the first time MAMA broadcast part of its award show from outside Asia in its twenty-five-year history. MAMA broadcast the remaining two days of the show from Osaka, Japan.

This collaboration between two cultures was a sign of how K-pop's influence has grown across the globe.

Millions of worldwide fans have embraced Korean language, food, and fashion as part of their love of K-pop. When MAMA announced the award for "APT," Bruno Mars thanked his fans in Korean onstage.

K-POP KICKS OFF

K-pop is short for "Korean popular music." K-pop can be an energetic dance song, a catchy pop tune, or a romantic ballad. This music blends multiple styles from around the world, ranging from hip-hop to reggae to salsa. But it can also include traditional Korean stories and instruments. Many K-pop artists sing in Korean and English.

K-pop started in South Korea in the early 1990s. South Korea is a small East Asian country, especially when compared to the United States. South Korea has about fifty-two million people. The United States has about 342 million people. South Korea is about the same size as the US state of Indiana. US culture played a big role in the beginning of K-pop.

From the 1960s to the 1980s, South Korea had a military-run government with strict censorship rules. This meant South Koreans could only enjoy media the government decided was patriotic. As a result, South Korean radio stations were not allowed to play many popular American songs. But in 1987, South Korea changed to a US-style democracy. The new government lifted some of the censorship rules.

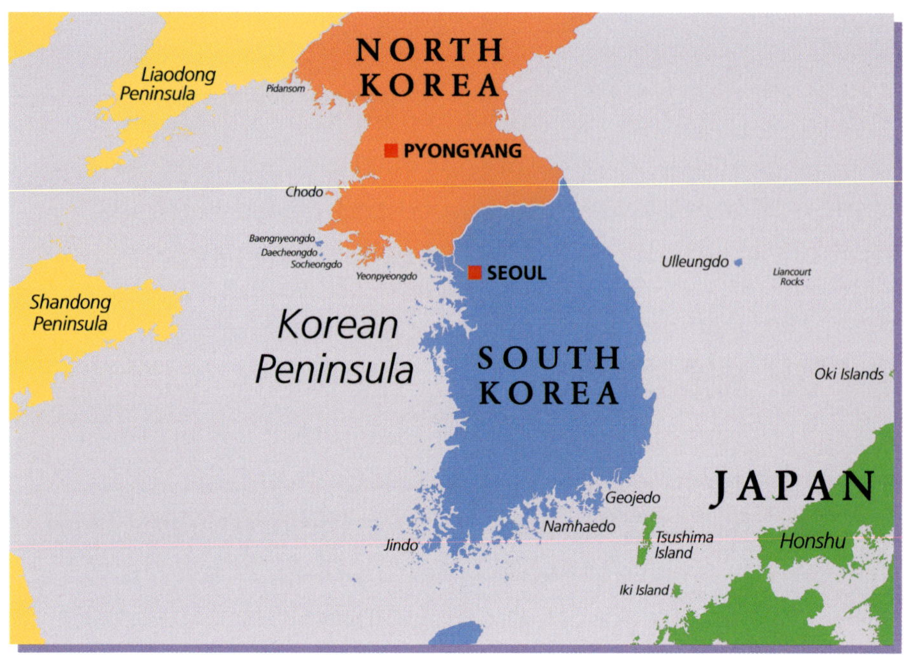

South Korea is located in the southern Korean Peninsula in East Asia.

South Koreans could now hear music from more countries. Some dance clubs in Seoul, the capital of South Korea, played American hip-hop songs. In 1992 South Korean singer Seo Taiji was seeking a new project. He and South Korean dancers Yang Hyun Suk and Lee Juno built the band Seo Taiji and Boys. Seo blended hip-hop and rock music for the group's songs. "[Seo's] music was sensational, it blew my mind," Yang said.

On a 1992 South Korean talent show, Seo Taiji and Boys sang "Nan Arayo (I Know)." The song mixed hip-hop, rap, rock, and techno music. All three performers had hip-hop style during their performances. Seo wore a shirt that looked like a New York Yankees baseball uniform. The group performed the song with several synchronized dance moves. It was the first time modern American pop music and Korean culture had been combined.

The talent show judges disliked the performance. They gave the group the lowest score. But young South Koreans loved this new sound. Teen fans bought over 1.5 million copies of the group's first album within one month of its release. Many of the group's song lyrics criticized the South Korean government and the remaining censorship laws. Fans looked up to Seo Taiji and Boys as leaders of Korean culture. The song "I Know" was the spark that lit the K-pop flame.

Seo Taiji and Boys performing at the Golden Disc Awards in 1993

KIMCHI CRAZE

Kimchi is a popular South Korean fermented food. It is made from cabbage, chili paste, garlic, and sometimes fish sauce. Before the 1988 Olympic Games in Seoul, kimchi was not well-known outside South Korea. Organizers made kimchi one of the official foods of the Olympic Village. Athletes loved kimchi and told the world. They helped kick off the global kimchi craze that continues today. BLACKPINK's Rosé shared her recipe for kimchi fried rice through *Vogue* magazine's social media. Kimchi fans put this traditional Korean dish on everything from pizza to hamburgers to hot dogs.

THE FIRST K-POP COMPANY

In the 1990s a music producer named Lee Soo-man was making plans to expand the scope of K-pop. Lee was a former Korean folk singer. He went to the United States when the South Korean government was censoring music. He got a degree in engineering at California State University, Northridge (CSUN).

While at CSUN, Lee witnessed the rise of MTV superstars such as Michael Jackson. MTV is an American cable television channel that got its start playing music videos. Lee returned to South Korea with the goal of producing Korea's own pop music superstars. He lost

Lee Soo-man speaks to business leaders at an event in Seoul in 2023.

money on the first singer he signed. But when he saw the success of Seo Taiji and Boys, he was determined to try again.

This time, Lee wanted a better way to train artists. He wanted to create perfect pop stars that teenage fans would idolize or adore. In 1995 he renamed his company SM Entertainment. Then he found talented singers and dancers. He spent many hours training them to become stars known as idols. Lee also hired songwriters and choreographers to help create a group's songs and dance moves. This system became the model for the K-pop industry.

H.O.T. was one of the most popular musical acts in South Korea in the late 1990s. The group disbanded in 2001.

In 1996 Lee created his first hit idol group. It was called H.O.T., which stands for High Five of Teenagers. This group is considered to be the first K-pop boy band. All five members of the group were born in South Korea. But member Tony An grew up in the United States.

The boy band's first album sold 1.5 million copies in 1996. Fans voted the group's song "Candy" the most popular song of 1996 in an Mnet music channel poll. Mnet is a South Korean music and entertainment channel. It has been broadcasting K-pop artists since 1995.

In 1998 H.O.T.'s techno dance song "We Are the Future" attracted K-pop fans outside South Korea. The video earned a nomination for the 1998 International Viewer's Choice award on MTV Asia. This former channel broadcast from Singapore to millions of fans in Southeast Asia.

Lee also created the first South Korean K-pop girl group, S.E.S. The letters stand for the names that the three members used onstage: Sea, Eugene, and Shoo. S.E.S. also attracted fans outside South Korea. In 1998 the group released its first Japanese single, "Into the New World." This song made it to number thirty-seven on the Oricon music chart in Japan.

K-BEAUTY FANS

K-pop idols have helped turn South Korean beauty products into a twelve-billion-dollar industry. Winter of the girl group aespa, for example, represents Korean beauty brand Espoir. Winter shares Espoir's eyeshadow and lipstick products through social media. US stars also share their love of Korean beauty products online. WNBA Chicago Sky forward Angel Reese made a video for *Vogue* magazine. Reese said she always wears Korean beauty brand Laneige, including during basketball games. She puts on the Laneige Lip Glowy Balm when she sits on the bench during breaks. "Whenever I get back to the bench [during] time-outs, the Laneige is on," Reese said.

Susan Kang, creator of Soompi, an online media company that covers Korean culture, said Lee is the person who turned producing K-pop into a science. Korean American Kang created Soompi in 1998. She ran it from her home in Los Angeles. Kang wanted a website where she and other fans could share news in English about their favorite K-pop idols. This was also one of the first fan websites to provide English translations of Korean entertainment articles. Lee's dream of spreading K-pop around the world was starting to become a reality.

K-POP AND THE KOREAN WAVE

Seo Taiji and Boys plus SM's early artists are part of K-pop's first generation. They also helped kick off South Korea's hallyu movement, or the Korean Wave. *Hallyu* refers to the spread of Korean music, food, and culture across the globe. In the late 1990s, two new K-pop companies helped build an even bigger wave. Former Seo Taiji and Boys dancer Yang Hyun Suk created YG Entertainment. Singer-songwriter Park Jin-young, better known as J. Y. Park, started JYP Entertainment.

Together, SM, YG, and JYP were called the "Big Three" K-pop companies in South Korea. These companies all trained their idols. But they each had a different focus. Lee hired international songwriters to help create unique K-pop songs. These songs blended pop, rock, and electronic dance music. Lee hired Norwegian songwriter Ziggy to create SM singer BoA's 2002 hit song "No. 1."

BoA is often referred to as the "Queen of K-pop" due to her long career and influence in the music industry.

Unlike SM, JYP's early K-pop groups reflected Park's musical tastes. He loved to blend American hip-hop, soul, and rhythm and blues (R&B) with Korean melodies. JYP signed rapper, singer, and hip-hop dancer Rain. This South Korean singer topped South Korea's music charts in 2002 with his first album, *Bad Guy*. Rain also expanded his popularity across Asia. He starred in the Korean television soap opera *Full House*. This show was broadcast in China, Japan, the Philippines, and more.

M IS FOR *MAKNAE*

In 2025 the *Oxford English Dictionary* (*OED*) added seven Korean words. These words included *maknae,* which means the youngest member of a family or K-pop group. *OED* is a global authority on the English language. Adding these words reflects the worldwide interest in Korean culture, media, fashion, and food. *OED* also added the food word *dalgona,* which is a honeycomb candy. Korean street vendors sell these flat disc candies, which have shapes such as hearts and stars carved into them. Korean kids make a game out of trying to cut out the shapes without cracking the delicate candies.

Similar to JYP, YG wanted to create K-pop groups with a bold, hip-hop vibe. But YG also helped set the stage for the catchy K-pop tunes of today. Yang mixed hip-hop beats with melodic choruses or hooks for fans to sing. The company displayed this style with groups such as 1TYM. This group of four male teens also blended Eastern and Western cultures. Two members were South Korean and two were Korean Americans from Los Angeles.

The group 1TYM also benefited from the beginnings of the internet. In the early 2000s, international K-pop fans could download 1TYM's MP3 music files from their own country. They used file-sharing websites such as Napster and LimeWire. These websites were huge for fans who had a hard time finding K-pop content in their home countries.

Worldwide K-pop fans also began to have closer contact with their idols. Before idols had social media profiles, fans could post messages for idols through fan cafés. These were hosted on Korean websites such as Daum. Fans could also chat with other K-pop fans. Soon the K-pop industry would be using the internet to help millions more people join the growing global fanbase.

Rain singing onstage for his comeback special on January 8, 2014

K-POP'S STAR RISES

In 2005 the new video-sharing platform YouTube helped K-pop make a bigger splash outside Asia. The K-pop industry used YouTube to post new music videos. Fans liked and shared videos to help rack up views for their favorite groups. Fans also posted translations of K-pop news and music. This helped other fans who did not know Korean join in the fun.

K-pop music videos helped fans get to know a group's sound, dance moves, and fashion. The members of the Wonder Girls were known for their retro sound and style. Their songs and outfits included elements of American 1960s R&B and 1970s disco. Their easy-to-learn dance moves created one of the first viral K-pop videos.

The Wonder Girls perform during the MTV World Stage Live in Malaysia 2010.

In 2007 their song "Tell Me" racked up millions of views worldwide. The Wonder Girls released an English version of their 2008 hit "Nobody." It became the first K-pop song to make it onto *Billboard*'s Hot 100.

The nine-member group Girls' Generation was popular for cheerful pop songs. The group's songs had catchy phrases fans could repeat. Girls' Generation also had fun dance moves. For example, they made a G with their hands in the video for their song "Gee." Their colorful skinny jeans set off a fashion trend. Girls' Generation was the first Asian girl group to have five music videos with over one hundred million views on YouTube.

Since Girls' Generation's debut, they have climbed the charts with hit songs such as "Run Devil Run," "Mr.Mr.," and "I Got a Boy."

The boy band SHINee was known for singing R&B songs. These songs harmoniously blended the voices of the five original members. Similar to Girls' Generation, SHINee also set fashion trends. Members wore skinny jeans with high-top sneakers and colorful sweaters. But SHINee showed a different dance style in their videos. They created choreography that included complex steps and jumps like a ballet. This boy band also racked up millions of YouTube views.

In 2013 SHINee had several comebacks in South Korea, including for their albums The Misconceptions of You, The Misconceptions of Me, *and* Everybody.

Both SHINee and Girls' Generation also gained popularity by appearing in Korean reality TV shows. *Hello Baby,* for example, featured Girls' Generation in 2009 and SHINee in 2010. The show had celebrities pretend to raise a toddler to see if they would be good future parents. Korean-speaking fans of these groups posted English translations of the shows on YouTube. This helped attract more fans outside South Korea.

As K-pop's popularity began to rise, South Korean technology brands helped spread the hallyu wave. The five members of the boy band BIGBANG were known for blending several styles. They mixed pop and hip-hop with styles such as country and electronic music. They also became fashion icons by dyeing their hair bright colors. In 2012 BIGBANG's videos had the highest number of international views on Google Korea's YouTube Korean language site. That same year, technology company Samsung Electronics sponsored BIGBANG's world tour. This tour included stops in the United States, Europe, and Asia.

YouTube helped many K-pop groups build bigger international fanbases. But it was a solo Korean artist who would soon gallop across the globe to make K-pop internet history.

K-POP CONQUERS THE WORLD

While YG's BIGBANG toured the world in 2012, YG was working with a South Korean rapper and singer who was about to make a bigger bang. PSY grew up in the wealthy Gangnam neighborhood in Seoul. He studied English and business in the United States. Then he decided to pursue a career in music back in his home country. PSY had some success in South Korea with more serious hip-hop songs. But in 2012 he released a humorous dance song called "Gangnam Style."

The video featured PSY doing a funny dance. He moved his legs as if he was riding a horse and moved his crossed wrists up and down. US celebrities such as pop singer Britney Spears shared the video. International fans created video tutorials on how to do PSY's dance. These posts helped "Gangnam Style" become the first YouTube video ever to get one billion views.

PSY performs "Gangnam Style" during an NFL halftime show in 2012.

PSY's smash hit in 2012 helped pave the way for the next huge international K-pop stars. While "Gangnam Style" was going global, a K-pop company called HYBE was working with a new boy band. Composer and music executive Bang Si-hyuk founded HYBE, which was first known as Big Hit Entertainment. Bang got his start as a composer for JYP. He wrote hit songs for acts such as Rain and the Wonder Girls.

In 2013 HYBE debuted BTS, one of the most successful K-pop groups in the world. BTS has seven members who all grew up in South Korea. The first

BTS is one of the most successful boy bands of all time with chart-topping records, brand ambassadorships, and UNICEF campaigns.

member that HYBE chose is the group's leader, a rapper named RM. He is fluent in English, which he learned by watching American TV show sitcoms. A few other BTS members speak some English. Most of the lyrics for BTS songs are in Korean.

But in 2020, BTS released a song with all-English lyrics called "Dynamite." This song became the first K-pop song to hit number one on *Billboard*'s Hot 100 chart in 2020. "Dynamite" also made BTS the first K-pop band to earn an American Grammy nomination in 2020.

At the same time, BTS was building up its popularity worldwide on HYBE's Weverse, a social media platform. BTS often replied to fan posts. They also collaborated with several international artists. These artists included

BTS performs "Butter" at the 2022 Grammy awards.

American rappers Nicki Minaj and Megan Thee Stallion. BTS also created songs with the American pop singer Halsey. BTS has worked with Chris Martin of the British rock group Coldplay as well.

BTS became so big that in 2019 the boy band generated $4.7 billion for South Korea's economy. The members of BTS have been global brand ambassadors for Korean brands such as Samsung Electronics and Hyundai Motor. In 2020 the government allowed BTS members to delay completing the eighteen-month military service required of South Korean men. In 2021 the government appointed BTS members as special presidential envoys to help promote South Korean culture worldwide.

While BTS was making its mark, YG's girl group BLACKPINK was also gaining global fame. The girl group has four members. Jisoo and Jennie were born in South Korea. LISA is from Thailand, and Rosé was born in Auckland, New Zealand. The group also speaks multiple languages, including Korean, Thai, Chinese, Japanese, and English.

In 2020 BLACKPINK became the first female K-pop group to win an MTV Video Music Award. It was for the song "How You Like That." In 2022 BLACKPINK released the album *Born Pink*. This album made BLACKPINK the first K-pop girl group to reach number one on *Billboard*'s Top 200 US albums chart. The group made history again in 2023 when BLACKPINK became the first Korean act to headline Coachella in California. This is one of the world's largest music festivals.

BLACKPINK headlines Coachella in 2023.

Looking back on "Gangnam Style" years later, PSY said he was happy that groups such as BTS and BLACKPINK were able to build on his success. "I think [BTS is] giving [Korea] a lot of proud moments," he said. "I feel very proud that I had a role in being that trigger. BTS have thanked me for that part several times, so I'm proud of it."

The massive success of K-pop acts such as PSY, BTS, and BLACKPINK would soon help other K-pop groups build armies of fans around the world. These groups and fans would show that they have power beyond just promoting music.

THE CARING K-POP COMMUNITY

BTS has nearly seventy-five million global members in its official fan club. The club is called ARMY, which stands for Adorable Representative M.C. for Youth. But fans do more than just post about their favorite BTS members. ARMY has many dedicated fans who translate BTS songs and videos. They post these translations for hundreds of thousands of fans who follow their social media. ARMY members also raise money in honor of BTS to support charity organizations around the globe.

Fans cheer as BTS performs in Central Park in New York City.

Australian high school teacher Jiye Kim became a BTS ARMY member after seeing her first BTS concert in Sydney, Australia. She loved the group's positive messages about community. Kim posts English translations of BTS content through social media. "I translate not for BTS, but [for] my fellow fans who through BTS find a sense of comfort or joy," Jiye said.

ARMY fans organize fundraisers to help support some of the same causes as BTS. In December 2024 ARMY fans in Los Angeles participated in an event with D'FESTA LA to raise funds for UNICEF. This United Nations agency provides education, nutrition, and health

In 2018 BTS spoke at the United Nations headquarters as part of their UNICEF campaign that advocates against youth violence.

services for children in nearly 190 countries. Together BTS and ARMY fans have raised about $6.6 million for UNICEF. The funds are part of BTS's "Love Myself" campaign to support children's mental health.

D'FESTA LA is the American location for a K-pop exhibit that started in South Korea and Japan. The exhibit features autographed photos, diary entries, and behind-the-scenes videos from some of today's most popular K-pop groups. These groups include BTS, TWICE, and Stray Kids.

TWICE is a diverse girl group with five Korean members, three Japanese members, and one Taiwanese member. A fan of TWICE is called a Once. These fans have raised thousands of dollars in TWICE's name to support such causes as children's health.

TWICE performing at Billboard's Women in Music event in 2023

K-POP FANS LET LOVE GLOW

At the 2024 Paris Olympics, the K-pop company HYBE helped Team Korea share a K-pop fan tradition with the world. HYBE worked with Korea's Olympic Committee to create nearly five thousand glowing light sticks. HYBE sent them to Team Korea for fans and athletes to wave at the Summer Games. K-pop fans wave light sticks with the official colors of their favorite K-pop groups at concerts. BIGBANG was one of the first K-pop groups to use light sticks. Fans waved yellow crown-shaped lights. At the Paris Olympics, fans waved light sticks inspired by the Olympic torch. HYBE's BSS, one of the subgroups of boy band SEVENTEEN, also led Team Korea in a cheer with its song "Fighting."

Light sticks are unique to each group and are customizable with stickers, beads, and ribbons.

Stray Kids performing during the MTV Video Music Awards in 2023

The boy band Stray Kids is another K-pop group whose fans have helped support children's health. Stray Kids has six members from South Korea and two members from Australia. JYP found the members through a reality TV show called *Stray Kids* that featured artists trying out for the group. Stray Kids' fans are called Stays. This represents how Stray Kids want fans to stay by their side. Stays have supported two of Stray Kids' causes, fighting childhood cancer and protecting the environment.

Together K-pop groups and their fandoms have shown they care by raising millions of dollars to support charities around the world. But sometimes the K-pop industry and its fans are not so kind.

K-POP CONTROVERSIES

K-pop has attracted more than 150 million fans around the world. Many fans love the positive messages of the music. They also love the sense of community they feel as members of fan clubs. But the pressures to be the perfect idol or even fan can be high.

BLACKPINK'S Rosé, for example, moved far away from her family in Australia when she was fifteen. She moved to South Korea to train with YG. To become an idol, she took vocal and dance lessons daily. She often practiced until late at night so she could become an outstanding singer and dancer. When she became an idol, she felt pressure to be perfect

Rosé is a global brand ambassador for Rimowa, a luxury German luggage brand.

when performing and responding to fans online. "We were trained to always present ourselves in the most perfect, *perfect* way," Rosé said.

These pressures are not new. K-pop idols have always trained hard to excel. What is new is that more idols have been talking publicly about these issues. Members of BTS have shared their struggles with anxiety, depression, and the stress of touring. TWICE member Mina took time off to deal with anxiety about performing onstage.

Karina performing at a music festival in 2023

Another tricky issue idols face is that some fans believe idols should not date. They believe idols should only love their fans. Karina, a member of SM's girl group aespa, faced this issue. When fans found out Karina was dating a Korean actor, some fans threatened SM by boycotting aespa's album. Karina posted a handwritten apology on Instagram and ended the relationship.

Fans can also cause problems for fellow K-pop fans. This trouble often happens in the form of cyberbullying, or online attacks. For example, members of one fandom may decide they don't like certain idols from other K-pop groups. These "antis" then show this dislike by posting insults of these idols and their fans through social media.

Some fans may even harass members of their own fandoms. This abuse has led some fans to create spaces where they feel safer. Some Black fans have

THE DAY K-POP STOPPED

On December 3, 2024, South Korea's President Yoon Suk Yeol declared martial law. Martial law means the military runs the government. The president said martial law was needed to protect South Korea from North Korea. North Korea is a communist country that is closed off and bans most foreign media such as K-pop.

K-pop fans around the world were shocked. K-pop events were canceled across the country. Some K-pop fans feared for idols who were serving in South Korea's military, including five BTS members. South Korea's politicians voted to end martial law on December 4. But hundreds of thousands of South Koreans gathered in Seoul to protest the president's actions. Many sang K-pop songs and waved light sticks with the colors of different K-pop fan groups.

joined online groups run by other Black fans. In the Philippines, a thirty-nine-year-old BTS ARMY member formed a Facebook group for older BTS fans after facing teasing for their age. The group is called Titas of BTS. *Titas* means "auntie" in the Filipino Tagalog language.

Despite the pressures, some idols are resisting the old rules. For example, many K-pop idols are not allowed to date or talk about dating, but in recent years, Rosé has been more candid with fans about her dating experience. Fans also find that the friends they make through the shared love of K-pop are worth overcoming any obstacles. In one interview, Demai Granali, founder of Titas of BTS, said she sees her group of Facebook friends as the greatest gift BTS ever gave her.

THE FUTURE OF K-POP

Evidence of K-pop's role in the global hallyu movement is everywhere. The US streaming service Netflix has a section dedicated to Korean content. It includes shows that Netflix helped produce, such as *XO, Kitty.* This show is full of K-pop hits from artists such as SEVENTEEN, BTS, BLACKPINK, and Stray Kids.

"I was really happy to know that they put all these really big K-pop songs in there, because K-pop has a huge worldwide following now and I'm proud of how well it's doing, as a Korean," actor Gia Kim said. Kim plays Yuri on the show. She has been a K-pop fan since she was a teen growing up in South Korea.

FANS FLOCK TO KCON

KCON is the world's largest K-pop convention and music festival. This event gives global K-pop fans the chance to see some of their favorite idols and learn more about Korean culture. In 2024 KCON Los Angeles hosted nearly six million fans. This number included fans who went to the festival and fans who watched online through KCON's digital platforms. Artists included international K-pop act KATSEYE. American music label Geffen Records and Korean K-pop company HYBE collaborated to create this six-member girl group. The diverse group has members who are Filipino, Korean, Swiss Ghanian, Venezuelan Cuban, Indian, and Chinese Singaporean. KCON started in Los Angeles in 2012 and has since expanded to such cities as Tokyo, Japan, and Bangkok, Thailand.

K-pop has also brought fans to South Korea to learn more about Korean culture. South Korea's government credited K-pop with helping bring in over six billion dollars in tourism in 2024. When tourists visit Seoul, they can enjoy several hallyu activities. These include K-beauty classes, Korean cooking classes, K-pop dance classes, and a tour of a kimchi museum.

Some K-pop industry experts wonder how long the K-pop boom will continue. In 2024 sales of physical K-pop albums in South Korea fell for the first time in ten years. But experts thought the fact that BTS and BLACKPINK were on breaks could have led to lower numbers. BTS members were completing their military service and BLACKPINK members were pursuing solo projects

The girl group aespa made it into the top ten in Korea's album sales in 2024. This is one of the groups helping to shape the future of K-pop. SM created aespa with four real members plus four avatars of these members. SM uses artificial intelligence technology to allow fans to have lifelike conversations with these avatars. Fans can communicate in English, Korean, or Japanese.

In early 2025 aespa set out to North America and Europe as part of their SYNK: PARALLEL LINE world tour.

Other companies are experimenting with all-virtual K-pop groups. PLAVE is a five-member virtual boy band. The members look like cartoons, but they have humans behind them. The agency Vlast had former K-pop idols who debuted but did not find success on their own help create PLAVE's songs and dances. In 2025 PLAVE had four songs on *Billboard*'s global charts. PLAVE also performed as part of the same MAMA show as Rosé and Bruno Mars.

Whether the future of K-pop will have real or virtual idols, or both, it seems the focus will remain on the music. K-pop started with South Korean artists gaining

LE SSERAFIM performs their hit song "Crazy" at the MTV European Music Awards in 2024.

inspiration from American music. The trend has since come full-circle. American songwriters now help create hits for K-pop artists. Universal Music Publishing Group (UMPG) hosts songwriting camps in Los Angeles to create new K-pop songs. UMPG pitches these new songs to K-pop companies, including HYBE, JYP, and SM.

One camp had songwriters from countries such as the United States, South Korea, and Germany. The group's writing credits included songs for BTS, TWICE, and LE SSERAFIM. Most of the songwriters at the camp did not start out writing K-pop. But now they enjoy writing in multiple musical styles, such as pop, rock, R&B, and hip-hop. "That's what I really love—you're not tied to anything," said songwriter Sandra Wikström, who is from Sweden. "I used to think, 'No, I don't want to do K-pop. I don't even know what K-pop is.' Then, I realized—K-pop is everything."

Important Dates

1987	South Korea adopts a US-style democracy and lifts some of its media censorship rules.
1992	Seo Taiji and Boys sing the first-ever K-pop song "I Know" on a talent show.
1995	Music producer Lee Soo-man creates South Korea's first K-pop company, SM Entertainment.
1996	Former Seo Taiji and Boys dancer Yang Hyun Suk starts YG Entertainment.
1997	Singer-songwriter Park Jin-young, better known as J. Y. Park, starts JYP Entertainment.
1998	Susan Kang creates Soompi, one of the first fan websites to translate K-pop lyrics into English.
2003	K-pop singer Rain stars in the K-drama *Full House,* building fans of Korean culture across Asia.
2007	K-pop group Wonder Girls has the first K-pop song ("Nobody") to make America's *Billboard* Hot 100.

2009	K-pop group Girls' Generation becomes the first Asian girl group to have five videos with over one hundred million views on YouTube.
2012	K-pop singer PSY's "Gangnam Style" becomes the first YouTube video ever to get one billion views.
2013	K-pop company HYBE debuts boy band BTS, one of the biggest-selling artists in K-pop history.
2019	BTS becomes the first K-pop group to earn an American Grammy nomination for the song "Dynamite."
2023	K-pop girl group BLACKPINK becomes the first Korean act to headline the US music festival Coachella.
2024	Mnet Asian Music Awards hosts part of its award show outside Asia for the first time.
2025	PLAVE, a five-member virtual boy band, has four songs on *Billboard*'s global charts.

Source Notes

8 Kim Jae-heun, "Rosé's 'Apt.' Redefines K-Pop's Global Appeal," *Korea Herald,* October 27, 2024, https://www.koreaherald.com/article/3833121.

10 Cho Chong-un, "K-Pop Still Feels Impact of Seo Taiji & Boys," *Korea Herald,* March 23, 2012, https://www.koreaherald.com/article/10359515.

15 Jenny Berg, "Angel Reese Reveals the K-Beauty Staple She Keeps on the Bench During WNBA Games," *Vogue,* January 8, 2025, https://www.vogue.com/article/beauty-secrets-angel-reese.

28 Rhian Daly, "PSY Says BTS Have Achieved 'Gangnam Style's 'Unfulfilled Dreams,'" *NME,* May 2, 2022, https://www.nme.com/news/music/psy-bts-achieved-gangnam-style-unfulfilled-dreams-3216886.

30 Inyoung Choi, "BTS Is One of the Biggest Music Sensations in History. Here's a Look Back on Their Meteoric Rise to Stardom," *Business Insider,* July 27, 2020, https://www.businessinsider.com/how-bts-became-global-sensation-popular-timeline

35 Lulu Garcia-Navarro, "The Interview: K-Pop Trained Rosé to Be 'a Perfect Girl.' Now She's Trying to Be Herself," *New York Times,* November 23, 2024, https://www.nytimes.com/2024/11/23/magazine/rose-blackpink-kpop.html.

37 Jean Bentley, "The 'XO, Kitty' Soundtrack Is Bursting With K-Pop Hits: Listen Here," TUDUM by Netflix, May 19, 2023, https://www.netflix.com/tudum/articles/xo-kitty-soundtrack-song-list-kpop.

41 Hannah Dailey, "Inside UMPG's Unlikely K-Pop Hit Factory," *Billboard,* August 22, 2024, https://www.billboard.com/music/features/kpop-songwriters-universal-music-publishing-group-international-songwriting-camp-1235757697/.

Selected Bibliography

Adams, Tim. "K-Everything: The Rise and Rise of Korean Culture." *Guardian.* September 4, 2022. https://www.theguardian.com/world/2022/sep/04/korea-culture-k-pop-music-film-tv-hallyu-v-and-a.

Bentley, Jean. "The 'XO, Kitty' Soundtrack Is Bursting With K-Pop Hits: Listen Here." TUDUM by Netflix. May 19, 2023. https://www.netflix.com/tudum/articles/xo-kitty-soundtrack-song-list-kpop.

BORA. "K-Pop's Hip-Hop Roots: A History of Cultural Connection on the Dancefloor." Grammy Awards. September 15, 2023. https://www.grammy.com/news/how-are-k-pop-hip-hop-connected-history-moon-night-club-idols-videos.

Dailey, Hannah. "Inside UMPG's Unlikely K-Pop Hit Factory." *Billboard.* August 22, 2024. https://www.billboard.com/music/features/kpop-songwriters-universal-music-publishing-group-international-songwriting-camp-1235757697/.

Kang, Liz. "'Gangnam Style' at 10: How PSY's Smash Hit Sent Korean Culture Global." CNN. July 14, 2022. https://www.cnn.com/style/article/psy-gangnam-style-10-years-intl-hnk/index.html.

Kim, Jae-heun. "Rosé's 'Apt.' Redefines K-Pop's Global Appeal." *Korea Herald.* October 27, 2024. https://www.koreaherald.com/article/3833121.

Liu, Marian Chia-Ming, Youjin Shin, and Shelly Tan. "How K-Pop Conquered the Universe." *Washington Post.* July 14, 2021. https://www.washingtonpost.com/arts-entertainment/interactive/2021/kpop-bts-youtube-twitter-blackpink/.

Moon, Kat. “Inside the BTS ARMY, the Devoted Fandom With an Unrivaled Level of Organization.” *Time.* November 18, 2020. https://time.com/5912998/bts-army/.

Romano, Aja. “How K-Pop Became a Global Phenomenon.” Vox. February 26, 2018. https://www.vox.com/culture/2018/2/16/16915672/what-is-kpop-history-explained.

Learn More

Becker, Trudy. *K-Pop.* Focus Readers, 2025.

Britannica: K-pop
https://www.britannica.com/art/K-pop

Britannica Kids: South Korea
https://kids.britannica.com/students/article/South-Korea/489861

Holleran, Leslie. *BTS: K-Pop's Biggest Headliners.* Lerner Publications, 2025.

Kiddle: BLACKPINK Facts for Kids
https://kids.kiddle.co/Blackpink

Layton, Christine. *Travel to South Korea.* Lerner Publications, 2024.

Index

Photo Acknowledgments

Image credits: Han Myung-Gu/Getty Images, pp. 6, 13, 34; Kevin Winter/Getty Images, p. 8; PeterHermesFurian/Getty Images, p. 10; JTBC PLUS/Getty Images, pp. 11, 14; Imaginechina Limited/Alamy, pp. 17, 21; AP Photo/Lee Young-ho/Sipa USA, pp. 19, 22; AP Photo/Lai Seng Sin, p. 20; Tom Szczerbowski/Getty Images, p. 24; Axelle/Bauer-Griffin/FilmMagic, p. 25; Chris Polk/Variety/Penske Media/Getty Images, p. 26; Frazer Harrison/Getty Images, p. 28; Drew Angerer/Getty Images, p. 29; The Asahi Shimbun/Getty Images, p. 30; Christopher Polk/Getty Images, p. 31; UPI/Alamy, p. 32; AP Photo/Charles Sykes/Invision, p. 33; AP Photo/Casey Flanigan/imageSPACE/Sipa USA, p. 35; david childers/Alamy, p. 39; Doug Peters/Alamy, p. 40.

Cover: Matt Winkelmeyer/Getty Images; Han Myung-Gu/Getty Images; Emma McIntyre/Getty Images.

Design element: Gregory Adams/Getty Images.